GW01239881

Eleanor Bron   *Joh*

Is Your Marriage Really Necessary?

Photographs by John Jefford

Eyre Methuen
London

1972

First published in 1972 by Eyre Methuen Ltd
11 New Fetter Lane, London EC4P 4EE
Copyright © 1972 by Eleanor Bron and John Fortune
Printed in Great Britain by Cox & Wyman Ltd, Fakenham, Norfolk

All the dialogues in this book were originally included
in the BBC television series *Where Was Spring?*
The illustrations for the two 'photoromances', *Pianissimo*
and *Love in the Big Top*, are reproduced by courtesy of the
BBC Television Graphics Department.

The quotation from 'Everyone Sang' on page 56 is reproduced from
Collected Poems 1908–1956 by Siegfried Sassoon, published by
Faber & Faber Ltd, by kind permission of G. T. Sassoon.

The photos on pages 49 and 54 are reproduced by courtesy of
Keystone Press Agency Ltd and Camera Press Ltd respectively.

SBN 413 29450 1

❧ Is your marriage really necessary!

Before

J: Please.   Please. . . .

E: You think if you say 'please' you can get anything you want.

J: No I don't, but I do think you're being ridiculously priggish.

E: I thought we both agreed to wait.

J: Oh good God, this is the twentieth century. It isn't as if we weren't engaged.

E: Look, darling, it's just as hard for me to wait as it is for you.

J: Are you worried about what people will say?

E: No, it just doesn't seem right, that's all.

Silence.

For Heaven's sake. Look – after we're married you can sleep with anyone you want. But until then, you sleep with me – understand?

✵Bed

J: Eleanor? . . .
E (*whispers*): Who is it?
J: Me.
E: Who?
J: John.
E: Which John?
J: Don John!
E (*giggles*): What do you want?
J: I'm lost. I can't find the way back to my bedroom.
E: I don't believe you!
J: Can I come in?
E: If you like.

JOHN *enters.*

J: Hallo.
E: Hallo. Are you coming to bed?
J: What! May I?
E: Don't turn the light on.
J: All right. Damn – this collar's stuck.
E: You've got a button off your shirt.
J: How do you know?
E: I couldn't take my eyes off it at dinner. I could see
   your chest.

4

J: I could see yours too, those see-through things are smashing.

E (*giggles*): They're all right.

J: I thought you were looking at me. I couldn't be sure. You've . . . Well . . .

E: I know – I've got a bit of a squint.

J (*laughs*): I find it terribly attractive. . . . Sorry I'm taking so long. . . .

E: Hasn't it been a super weekend?

J: Sensational. It's getting better and better.

E: You are a slowcoach! What are you doing?

J: Just taking my trousers off. It's so dark. Bloody zip. . . . (*Sound of ripping cloth.*) Oh . . . well . . . that takes care of that.

E: About time. We can't wait forever can we?

J: Here I am. (*He comes over to the bed.*) I've been sitting in my room for two hours, trying to pluck up courage. . . . I thought you wanted me to come but I wasn't sure.

E: I hoped you would. Come on then what are you waiting for?

J (*crossing to the bed*): This is awfully decent of you. . . . Darling.

E: Not at all. . . . You do know Robert don't you?

❧ In the Cairngorms

JOHN *has belayed on a ledge.*
He shouts instructions to Eleanor,
who is struggling up towards him.

J: Take in, take in!

E: I daren't let go. Couldn't you pull me up, John?

J: It's against all the principles.

E: No one will ever know.

J: Try. . . . There's a handhold *there* – no, to the left a little. Fine. You're doing fine, Eleanor.

E: Wow!

J: Good girl. . . . Aren't you proud of yourself? Now just catch your breath and we'll go on.

E: Oh. John let's stop here for a minute.

J: We ought to push on up.

E: What was it you wanted to tell me?

J: Oh. When we get to the top.

E: I don't think I'll ever get to the top.

J: It's a beautiful view. You can't miss that.

E: Why do you have to tell me here?

J: I didn't want us to be interrupted.

E: John, I've no idea what it is, but if it's what I think it might be, I mean, we've got to go all the way down again.

J: We're here now.

7

He turns and starts to look for footholds.

Eleanor?

E (*sighs*): Yes.

J: Eleanor. How shall I put this?

E: Knock it into that crack, look.

J: Oh, I hadn't seen it. Well done! You see! . . . The thing is, we've been seeing each other for four years now. You must have wondered why I've never told you I love you.

E: No, I haven't.

J: You must have. You see, it is a difficult thing to say to someone – I love you.

E (*pained*): Do you John?

J: No – I was just saying, it's a difficult thing to say. That isn't why I've never said it. The reason I've never said it is that I don't love you. I like you very much. I think you're wonderful. I hate to think I might be wasting your time when you could be –

E: Oh, what a relief! I was so afraid you'd hauled me up this mountain so you could ask me to marry you.

J: So you don't mind? You're not hurt?

E: Oh John. I was so dreading hurting you.

J: You couldn't hurt me. That's wonderful. It puts our relationship on a new footing. Now we know where we stand.

E: We'll still be friends.

J: More than ever.

With great difficulty he kisses her.

E: But I think we shouldn't sleep with each other any more.

J: I quite agree. To be honest, I never really enjoyed it.

E: Nor did I. What a relief!

J: It's a weight off my mind.

They shoot up the mountain face and clamber over the top.

Look at that view . . . Oh. Well. You can imagine what it would be like . . .

E: Without the fog.

J: Yes. Just a minute. (*He rummages in his rucksack and produces a postcard.*) It's roughly like that.

E: It must be lovely. . . . It is nice not to have to pretend any more.

J: Isn't it funny how things turn out? I mean I thought I was going to fall for you very early on but I didn't. If I saw you when I wasn't expecting it, I used to get that funny feeling in the pit of my stomach.

E: Yes – I know. I thought I would fall in love with you too. I couldn't think of anything wrong with you.

J: Oh nonsense. There's plenty wrong with me.

E: Oh, I know. Of course. But I didn't know you terribly well then. I soon realized it wouldn't work. It's a pity, because it would have been perfect. You do have all the qualities I look for, and you're one of the few people I can talk to.

J: Did you really think that's why I was bringing you up here, to ask you to marry me?

E: Well, I did and I didn't. My mother did, of course. That's why she sends you sheets every Christmas. She'll be a little upset.

J: I'll send them back.

E: Don't be silly.

J: What would you have said?

E: What?

J: If I had asked you.

E: If you had? . . . Well. I don't know. If I thought you wanted it – you ought to be married you know – I think I'd have said 'Yes'.

J: Well. Will you?

E: What?

J: Marry me?

E: Don't be ridiculous.

J: Please.

E: No.

J: Why?

E: No. I'm too romantic.

J: We both are. But the ideal person may never come along.

E: Well. *Then* I'll marry you.

An ocean liner. Sunset. The first night at sea. ELEANOR *and* JOHN *leaning on the ship's rail.*

J: How far do you go?

E: All the way. You?

J: The same . . . Brindisi.

E: Oh, good.

J: What's your cabin like?

E: Fine. It's nice not to have to share at this time of year.

J: Mm. It's wonderful to find someone to talk to. Makes the journey seem much shorter.

E: It is shorter now . . . they've changed the route.

J: Have they? (*Laughs.*) And it's such a change to talk to someone civilized. . . . Talking about civilization . . . and just as a matter of interest . . . you're a woman . . . what d'you think about the Pill?

E: Why?

J: Well . . . you know, one does hear . . . you know, drugs and all that . . . of course I wouldn't know, but one does hear there are certain side effects. . . .

E: Well, there probably are. But the damn things are so convenient.

J: Exactly. Good.

E: Of course, it does still leave the responsibility with the woman. . . .

J: Oh, I don't know. I think it's up to the man too . . . I still rely on the old fashioned condoms. . . .

E: Really? Are they still used?

J: Very much so. They're still very, very popular. I imagine the barman has stacks of them.

E: I would never have known. I've never gone into these things, of course . . . but times have changed, haven't they?

J: Oh, I agree. Yes, one of the effects of the Pill has been to make women free . . . now that the fear of social consequences is out of the way.

E: Yes, . . . I suppose it means that a lot of women won't feel so inhibited . . . haven't you found that?

J: Mmmm . . . well no, not really – to a certain extent perhaps.

E: Mind you, it does depend entirely on how much a woman wants it. I mean, Pill or no Pill, there are some women who simply can't do without. Haven't you found that?

J: Mmmmm Mmmm . . . go on . . . are you in that category?

E (*thinks*): Mmm. Yes I suppose I am. The whole thing about men wanting it more than women is a lot of balls . . . and personally I find – and I'm sure you do – I can tell within five minutes whether I'm going to be attracted to a man.

If I want to go to bed with a man I never leave him in any doubt at all.

J (*anxious*): Oh . . . really?

E: None at all!

J: Well that's marvellous.

E: One thing actually – now you mention it –

J: What.

E: Side effects of the Pill. I think, you know, that it does diminish desire . . . It must be some kind of depressant.

J: Yes . . . well, that is rather depressing.

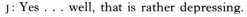

Before the Wedding

JOHN *and* ELEANOR *in bed, curled up asleep. A pause.*

E (*wakes up*): . . . John?

J: Good morning darling. . . .

He gives her a sleepy kiss.

E: Hallo! (*She laughs.*) Darling?

J: Mmm . . . ?

E: Do you know what day it is today?

J: Mmhmm.

E (*snuggles up to him*): What time is it?

J: Mm? . . . Oh . . . Quarter . . . past nine. . . .

E: What! No! – The bridesmaids are supposed to be here at ten. Oh help! John. Get up! . . . This thing must have gone wrong. (*She looks at the tea-maker alarm.*) John! You're crazy.

J: Why?

E: Fool! It's not quarter past nine. It's six o'clock.

J: Oh . . . sorry. Well turn it back to six o'clock and let's have a cup of tea. Where did that come from?

E: My sister.

J: Angela?

E: Yes. Didn't I show it to you? It was her wedding present.

J: Jolly nice too. I didn't know air hostesses did so well for themselves.

E: Did I tell you Mummy phoned last night? She's so sentimental. She was very worried.

J: Why?

E: Oh. She said she didn't like the idea of my spending my 'last night alone' alone. (*They laugh.*) If she could see us now! I've heard so many of my friends who've been living together say that as soon as they decided to get married everything went wrong . . . but it seems to have made us – much better. Hasn't it?

J: Mm. Much.

E: Mmm . . . do you want to see my wedding dress? . . .
   I'm going to try it on!

J: Hey! I thought it was supposed to be unlucky to see
   the bride in her dress.

E: Silly, that only applies to the groom!

J: Oh yes.

E: It is a bore. I wish we could have got married on the
   same day.

J: Never mind. At least I'll be there. Besides, I wanted
   to be Edward's best man. I couldn't do both.

E: He insisted on a white wedding you know. I was
   surprised.

J: Ah well, it's all for the best. . . .

E: All for the best man, actually!

They laugh variously.

13

It's worked out terribly well hasn't it?

J: Well, of course. It's what I said: if we hadn't decided to get married we'd never have stayed together. We were going from bad to worse! Physically and mentally: it was humdrum, man. That's the only word for it. We might just as well have been married . . . Now – well! We'll have all the excitement: the danger, the thrills, letters, clandestine meetings . . . All the advantages of Adultery.

E: Ooh that word . . . it gives me goose pimples . . . look!

J: I mean, it's already so much better.

E: Yes. . . . And this is just *pre*marital infidelity!

J: Yes! And think – when we're married, even at your home, even in office hours, there's always a chance that Edward will turn up unexpectedly. Does he get migraine or anything like that?

E: I don't know. You probably know him better than I do. He's terribly conventional.

J: That's all to the good. He'll be jealous then. Such a big man, all that red hair. I should imagine he's given to uncontrollable rages.

E: Mmm, . . . I'm a bit afraid he'll be rather possessive. What if he did come back and find us?

J: But that's just it!

E: Darling! He might shoot you, and I couldn't bear it!

She hugs him.

J: Has he got a gun?

E: Yes.

J: Marvellous. What kind?

E: Ooh I don't know. It's a . . . Russian, I think, em . . . begins with an S . . . Sawnoff?

J: Sawnoff . . . Sawnoff shotgun!

E: Yes, I think so. Are they good?

J: What on earth does he want with one of those?

E: He goes out at night, he says, hunting.

J: What?

E: Owls, he said, or something.

J: In the middle of Mayfair?

E: I don't know. Maybe. There are nightingales in

Berkeley Square. I'm counting the days to your wedding. She's a very lucky girl, Cynthia.

J: Edward's a lucky man.

E: She's awfully pretty, Cynthia. She and my sister Angela were at school together.

J: Yes she told me.

E: Which do you think is more beautiful? Cynthia or Angie?

J: There's not much in it. . . .

E: I've always been jealous of Angela, you know.

J: Why?!

E: She is so lovely. The odd thing is she doesn't have any man at all, that I know of. I suppose because she's always on the move; she never has time.

J: Oh I don't know. It doesn't take all that long.

The door buzzer goes.

E: God! Who can that be?

J: Who can it be? It's the front door. Is it the bridesmaids?

E: It's much too early. It certainly can't be Edward. It must be my mother.

J: Oh for God's sake!

He gets out of bed.

E: Oh for God's sake!

The buzzer goes.

J: Where are my trousers . . . ?

E: I'll have to open it! . . .

J: Wait a minute! . . . (*Putting on his shirt.*) . . . Wait a minute!

E: Hurry up!!! Hurry UP!

J (*tying his tie*): I am. . . . Tell her to go away!

E: I can't! It's my wedding . . .

J: Oh God. . . . My tie. Eleanor, my tie – I can't –

E: It doesn't matter about your tie! For God's sake – get your trousers on! (*Buzzer.*) I'll have to answer it . . . What shall we say? . . . (*Buzzer. She goes to the phone and picks it up.*)

J: Sound sleepy.

E: Hallo? . . . Who is it? . . . Yes I was. Is that Mummy?

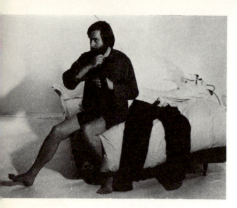

... Oh for God's sake – I thought it was Mummy! Come up! (*She hangs up.*) Phew! ... It's all right, it isn't.

J: Thank God for that. . . . Who is it?

E: My sister – Angela.

J: Angela! Oh my God!

E: What's the matter?

J: Oh my God. Is she coming up?

E: Yes.

J: Why didn't you tell her to go away?

E: She's only just got back.

J: Oh no . . . no!

E: Don't be silly. She won't think anything. Say you've come round for the ring.

J: At six-thirty?

E: She never has any idea what country it is, let alone what time.

J: She mustn't find me here. It'll be the end of everything.

E: What do you mean. . . . Oh no. . . . No. Oh no! No! Oh no!

J: Angela – I mean Eleanor – listen to me darling – I love you.

E: Don't touch me. . . . You and Angela. My God, what a blind fool I've been! How could you?

J: I don't care about her.

E: She's my sister.

J: Exactly! That's what made it so exciting. I knew how desperately wounded you'd be if you found out.

E: What about Cynthia? Wasn't that enough for you?

J: I'm not in love with Cynthia. It doesn't mean anything to me to deceive her. But deceiving you! That was a terrifying, wonderful risk! I couldn't resist it.

E: Then we might just as well have got married.

J: Don't say that!

E: But it's true. . . . Go away . . . leave me now.

J: Eleanor . . .

E: Go now . . . I hope you realize that you've ruined the happiest day of my life . . .

J (*going*): Goodbye. . . . See you in Church.

During

❧ In the hotel

A bedroom in Athens. JOHN *is standing by the bed, very happy and relaxed.*

J (*agreeing*): I *did* enjoy it! It was a super wedding. Best wedding I've ever been to. (*Laughs.*) Your parents really did us proud. . . . Darling? What are you doing? Are you coming to bed? . . .

E (*calling, slightly flustered*): Just a minute darling . . .

J: I'm waiting . . .!

E: Just a minute darling . . . I'm having a bit of . . . Ah! . . .

She enters.

J: Ah *enfin*!

E: Close your eyes.

J: Come on darling. We haven't got all day. . . .

E: Yes we have if we want. (*She sits on the bed.*)

J: Not if we're going to get to Sparta by lunch.

E: I do love you darling. . . . Are you happy?

J: Oh! I'm absolutely bursting. I haven't felt so excited since I was thirteen. I don't think I'm going to be able to sleep at all.

E: Aren't you?

J: Darling – there are so many things I want to show you. You've got a lot to learn you know.

E: Oh John. I know I have . . . I want to learn, my love. And only you can teach me how.

J: Eleanor. I'm so excited . . . I can hardly wait for
tomorrow. I've worked out a marvellous route. . . .
We'll start at Epidaurus and we should be able to
have a quick look at Olympia on the way down to
Mistra.

E: Lovely. . . . (*She gets into bed.*) Oh – this is a nice
bed . . .

J: Excellent. Greek beds always are. It's a lovely
room. . . . What a good idea it was to fly out here.
Wouldn't have occurred to me. Of course, I usually
come by train . . . but a honeymoon is rather special.

E (*laughs*): It would have been awful to spend our first
evening in London.

J: Yes. . . . Hey – what's that you're wearing?

E (*blushes*): What? Do you like it? (*She pushes the
blanket down.*) It's a nightdress.

J: Beautiful. . . . Beautiful. . . . You know what it is of
course?

E: What?

J (*pulling the blanket up*): It's a chiton.

E: A what?

J: A chiton. C.H.I.T.O.N. On all the statues. You'll
see dozens of them tomorrow . . . Darling . . . You
are such a beautiful thing. (*Kisses her.*) You look like
the Satallan Aphrodite . . . I wish I could show her to

you, but we haven't time . . . still – we must be grateful for whatever we can cram in.

E: I'm so glad we decided to come to Greece.

J: It's all worked out marvellously. I could never have justified taking two weeks' holiday from the thesis. But a honeymoon! That's quite a different matter. It was a wonderful idea of yours Eleanor!

E: Good.

J: Tomorrow my darling, if we wake up early enough we can see the dawn over the Acropolis. (*Kisses her.*) It's the most romantic sight in the whole world. (*Breathes deeply.*) Smell that air . . . Isn't it incredible. I'm going to sleep like a top . . . (*Drowsily into his pillow.*) Goodnight darling wife.

E: I don't think I'm going to sleep at all.

J: Oh. Well if you want something to read in the night I've put Kitto's *The Greeks* by your bed . . . you can do some background reading.

E: I took a pill. . . .

J: Oh well then. Nothing to worry about. . . . (*He sleeps.*)

E: It was to keep awake.

ELEANOR *and* JOHN *in bed. Strained silence.*

E (*sighs*): . . . How long are we going to go on like this?
J: What?
E: Oh! Come on!

JOHN *shrugs.*

E: Oh! Let's not pretend!
J (*smiles*): Mmm?
E: Oh John. Isn't it time we stopped lying to each
other?
J: No . . . not yet.

✳ Knitting

J: . . . And so, you see, I thought we ought to talk about it.

E (*concentrating on her work*): Yes. . . .

J: You're not listening to me, are you?

E (*indignantly*): Yes.

J: Then what do you think?

E: What? Just a minute, darling.

She refers to her pattern.

J: Darling, I wish you'd take a bit of notice of me.

E: Yes. (*She glances at the knitting, then at the pattern.*) Oh, I see . . .

J: Honestly. Sometimes I feel like a fly on the wall.

E: You know where the fly spray is, darling . . .

J: Eleanor!

E: Yes. . . ?

J: I'm sorry, but I really think you ought to . . . see a psychiatrist. . . .

E: Who?

J: You.

E: Me?

J: Yes, darling.

E: Or you?

J: No. You.

E: A psychiatrist. . . ? Why?

J: I don't seem to be able to get through to you any more.

E (*smiling, knitting*): Mm . . . Mmm . . .

J: It's been going on for months now. It's just as if I didn't matter to you any more, as if I . . . didn't exist. I can't understand it. We always had so much to talk about. That's what I loved about you . . . your vivacity . . . gaiety. . . .

E (*gaily*): Yes!

J: Is it I who have changed. . . . Is it?

E: Probably darling. Sorry, I've got to a tricky bit. . . . (*Consulting her pattern.*)

J: Look, Eleanor. For God's sake. Stop doing that and give *me* some attention. Put that *down*.

E: But this is for you, darling!

❧ Our tune

JOHN *and* ELEANOR *have come out into the night air to sit out the next dance.*

J: Happy, darling?
E: Mmm . . . You? . . .
J: What do you think? . . .

The music changes.

E: Darling?
J: Mmmm.
E: Can you hear? . . .
J: What?
E: Listen . . .
J: What?
E: What they're playing.
J: Yes. . . ?
E: Darling! – They're playing our tune!

J: No they're not.

E: What do you mean?

J: This isn't it. This is 'Moon River'. 'Buttons and Bows' is our tune.

E: 'Buttons and Bows' darling?

J: Just a minute . . .

He strikes a match.

J:
E: } Who the hell are you?!

At the cheese counter

E: Excuse me.
(*Laughing*.)
I think *I* was
before you!

J: Please. Go on.
I am sorry.

E: I was before you, wasn't I? I *think* I was. I only want
one thing, actually. I'm in rather a hurry.

J: Most of us only want one thing.

E: I beg your pardon?

J: I said most of us only want one thing. I only want one
thing, but it doesn't look as if you're going to give it
to me.

E: Oh. I see. (*She gives her order*.) One pound of
double Gloucester cheese, please. (*She takes the
cheese*.) Thank you. (*Remembers*.) Oh and . . . (*Sees
JOHN.*) Oh, after you. . . .

J (*to a second assistant*): Have you got any double
Gloucester cheese? . . . No? Oh, I see. Thank you.

E: Oh dear. I seem to have taken it all. I am sorry. But I
was before you, you know.

J: No you weren't. You see, I've been here for an hour
and a half.

E: An hour and a half? That's not possible, surely?

J: Oh yes. Ladies first, you see.

E: Well, that's certainly very polite.

J: Oh, it's not just politeness. One must put others first.

E (*laughs*): If everyone did that no one would get any-
where!

J: I'm sorry you said that. Are you a Christian?

E: Well. You know . . .

25

J: Yes I do know. I've been trying to live according to Christian principles, but I don't think they work.

E: Oh dear. You mustn't let yourself get downhearted over a piece of cheese.

J: It's not just the cheese. But I'm late for work now, you see. I've been here for an hour and a half. I'll get the sack this time. It's inevitable.

E: Oh surely not. . . .

J: Oh yes. I don't know how I'm going to tell the children. I've got rather a lot. My wife's a saint. She stays in bed all day. I have to ask myself whether I would be right to send Bridget – she's my eldest – on the streets. Not for myself, you understand, but for the others. Of course, prostitutes do fulfil certain needs – I'd be the last to cast the first stone.

E: You always seem to be the last.

J: Give me the cheese.

E: I beg your pardon?

J: Give me the cheese.

E: That's not a very Christian thing to say.

J: I'm through with Christianity. I've lost my job. My daughter's going to leave university and take up prostitution. I have to do all the housework.

E: I'm very sorry. But why this mania for my piece of cheese?

J: Let's forget about it. The cheese is not all that important. I just wish I could find something, someone to give me hope. That's all I want. Well . . . now I'd better go off and get the sack.

E: Oh, but that's terrible. I wish there were something I could do. . . . (JOHN *looks at her.*) Besides I need it. This evening. You might have made all this up. For all I know you're a very rich man having a joke at my expense.

J: I don't understand, you see. I'm flummoxed. If I hadn't kept giving up my place to ladies who came in after me, I'd have the cheese, I'd have my job, Bridget would get her degree . . . it's all too complicated for me.

ELEANOR *tries to give him some money. He refuses.*

26

I don't want money.
I *do* want the cheese.

E: Please. Let's try to be adult about it.

J: 'But whosoever shall compel thee to go a mile, go with him twain.'

E: Oh, for heaven's sake, Here –
She gives him the cheese.

J: Oh . . . I . . .
He is overcome.

E: Tch. This is ridiculous! It's only a piece of cheese!

Snatching back the cheese, she storms off.

✿ Geoffrey

E : How's it going, darling?
J : Rather well I think. I'm just
    working on your darling little
    nose.
E : You remember the other night
    you asked me what Geoffrey
    could give me that you can't?
J : Yes.
E : Well I've made a list. . . .

✤ In the bedroom

JOHN *and* ELEANOR *waking up in their wrecked bedroom.*

J: What time is it?

E: Ah . . . we'll have to get another clock.

J: Can't afford it. I'll phone TIM.

E: We can't afford that either. Would you like a nice cup of tea?

They laugh.

J: I'll get it.

E: No. I'll get it.

They stay put.

How do you feel?

J: Happy Anniversary darling.

E: Oh darling, don't.

J: No, I mean it. This is the first day of our second year together. It's going to be wonderful. Last night was painful, but I think it taught us both a lot.

E: Darling, there's blood on your pillow!

J: Just a scratch.

E: I'm sorry. (*She kisses it better.*)

J: Ouch! I feel I know you so much better today – after last night – and indeed myself. I think it was wonderful of you to put up with me for a whole year.

29

E: I think we both had a lot to put up with, frankly, darling. We'll have another party tonight – only this time it'll be a real celebration. And this time I won't drink anything . . .

J: Nonsense! Just have to go a bit easy, that's all.

E: I didn't mean any of those things I said to you last night.

J: Neither did I. I was beastly.

E: No you weren't. Everything you said was true. I learned so much from it.

J (*gloomily*): So did I.

E: And don't start getting depressed.

J: No, I'm not really. . . .

E: You know me – when I start screaming I'll say anything. You have to realize – there's a good and a bad side to everything.

J: Yeah . . . I'd like to know what's the good side of being – what did you call me? 'An ageing narcissus without the equipment.'

E: But – I didn't mean it, darling. You're not vain.

J: Yes I am. I realized it last night. (*To the mirror.*) That is the face of a vain man.

E: Don't start getting depressed, darling. . . .

J: 'Vanity of vanities, saith the preacher, all is vanity.' How disgusting!

E: I think you've got a very interesting face.

J: It's an appalling face. I'm fascinated by its ugliness – Oh God . . .

ELEANOR *starts to sing 'Hearts and Flowers'.*

Darling, don't do that, please . . .

She goes on.

Please, don't, darling – it's silly.

She goes on.

SHUT UP!

E: You shut up! I'm glad I told you – instead of bottling it up. Every time I want to go to the bathroom, you're in there plucking your eyebrows.

J: Well, otherwise they'd grow right across in a straight line . . . that's horrible . . . I'm completely horrible – I don't see how you can live with me.

E: Don't start up your self-pity – please.

J: Yes, you told me about that too. Self-pity – how I despise that in myself. I'm disgusting.

E: Nonsense.

J: I disgust you too.

E: Now you're exaggerating. . . .

J: Well, I do. You said so.

E: Look darling, you said some pretty awful things to me last night you know . . . you don't see me sitting down and wallowing. God! Do you realize how lucky we are? I mean, do you have any idea how few people have the chance to know themselves – really know themselves? I'm surprised you don't value that, being so vain . . . I'm going to try to learn from what you said to *me* . . . or rather shouted at me . . . I can't pretend I like to be compared to a Dachau camp guard . . . I'm sorry if you think I'm a racist.

J: I never said that darling, I said sadist.

E: Well if you didn't say it you certainly implied it . . . why drag in Dachau?

J: It's an ordinary everyday example of sadistic cruelty.

E: Oh come on darling. For you to say that to me? You know it doesn't make the slightest difference to me that you're Jewish. But all Jewish people are far too sensitive, you indulge in a kind of cosmic self-pity, when it would be much better just to forget the whole thing and start again.

J: But you know I don't even think of myself as Jewish.

E: Well you are darling. You can't help it. Marrying me didn't alter anything . . . your family certainly think of you as Jewish – that's why they're not speaking to you.

J: Oh Christ!

E: There you are – you're sorry for yourself. You see, at least I don't – and you do, my darling – let my masochistic side get the upper hand.

J: Well, if I am a masochist, I certainly married the right woman.

E: Well – perhaps I am a sadist . . . you're probably right – if that's what you call telling the truth. It just seems to me that it's my duty, as your wife, to point out a few little things. You could be so wonderful.

J: If I weren't such a capon. . . .

E: If you like. But I don't think I get any perverse gratification from telling you these things and, even if I did, I should still feel I had to tell you – whatever my real motives – because I'm a very honest person.

J: Yes, you're one of those honest people who can't bear to hear the truth.

E: I don't mind the truth. Huh, you call *me* sadistic. What you said to me was unforgivable – a complete betrayal. . . .

J: What – how??

E: You know – that dig about ending up like Joanna.

J: Oh, come on, your mother's a *real* alcoholic, darling. You couldn't be like her, not in a million years. She's drinking a bottle of gin a day. For one thing, you drink whisky – and anyway you could stop any time you wanted to.

E: Of course I can.

J: Of course. And even at your worst you're still pretty coherent.

E: Thank you very much.

J: Well honestly, you are.

He kisses her.

J: I'll tell you what – why don't we stay in bed all day – really celebrate?

E: No thank you. It seems I'm not much use in that department.

J: Oh – that. Darling, I was joking. . . .

E: No you weren't. There's nothing funny about frigidity. I thought it was rather cheap. . . .

J: Anyway, you're not frigid, deep down. Certainly not when you've got half a bottle of whisky inside you. Come on, give me a kiss. Would you like some whisky?

E: No thanks.

J: Darling, I love you. We've had a row . . .

E: Our first!

J: . . . but that was good – things will be much better from now on.

E: Yes. I love you too. At least, if we didn't love each other we shouldn't be able to hurt one another as much as we do. . . .

After

✿ God speaks through a hole in the wall

JOHN *and* ELEANOR *carrying a step-ladder. They stop at Simon's door, and try the handle. It is locked. They put down the ladder.* JOHN *climbs up.*

J: Simon? Can you hear me? This is God speaking.

E (*whispering*): Disguise your voice!

J (*whispering*): I am disguising my voice.

E (*whispering*): You'll have to do better than that!

J: Look – am I God or are you? Sorry about that, Simon. As I was saying, this is God speaking. Look – I want you to snap out of this, Simon. I want you to unlock your door like a good boy, and come downstairs and have your meals with the rest of us – I mean with your father and mother and Rufus and . . . Yes, but you see Simon, grown-up people can't really manage on seven grains of rice a day. . . . Well if your Daddy promises faithfully to try to eat only seven grains of rice, can he smoke a cigarette – just one? . . . No, he won't catch cancer – I'll keep an eye on him. I want you to bear in mind that your not eating isn't going to help the children starving in China – I wish I hadn't told you about them – I mean I wish your father had never mentioned it. . . . (*To* ELEANOR.) Can't catch what he's saying. . . .

E: He says your voice sounds just like his father's.

J: Doesn't that make your father a nicer man – that he sounds like God? And while we're on the subject Simon – don't you think you're a bit hard on him? And on your mother too? They can't help knowing that you think they're wicked – and it hurts them dreadfully. . . . Yes, I'm listening. . . . Want to kill who? . . . No, that doesn't make you a monster Simon, every little boy wants to kill his father. You wouldn't be normal if you didn't. . . . And to what? . . . Yes, well that's perfectly natural too,

especially if she's young and attractive, like your mother. . . . What?

E (*jumping up*): It's no good to keep on asking why you were born Simon . . . Oh – sorry . . . er this is God's Mummy speaking. Now that you're here, you'll just have to put up with it like everybody else does. . . . What? . . . You're swallowing your words, Simon – try to enunciate. . . .

J: I think he's crying. . . .

E: Oh God . . .

J: Tell him the joke about the elephant.

E: Which one?

J: The one about Tarzan.

E: Uh . . . God has asked me to ask you if you know what Tarzan said when he saw the elephants. . . . Yes, that's right! Simon do stop crying. . . . He says he can't stop crying, because he's guilty. . . .

J (*jumps up*): It's no use trying to take the sins of the world on your shoulders, Simon. You're not guilty, you're not anything. . . . I mean – I don't mean you're nothing . . .

E: Simon? You're not nearly old enough to be guilty – you only get guilty when you grow up. . . . No. That isn't a reason not to want to grow up! The only thing that makes me rather cross, Simon, is that you're not happy. God and I are rather sad that you don't seem to like your new bicycle – and all those other lovely toys that lots of little children who are less fortunate than you would be glad of. Daddy worked so hard to send you to the Mound, and now you won't go back. . . . It's a splendid school, Simon, and you know you simply can't get the grounding for Chartered Accountancy in a Seminary. Simon, do be reasonable. Daddy's been quite ill with worry, he nearly died. . . .

J: Yes, of course he'll go to heaven – come to heaven. . . . Yes! Quite possibly in an old Bath Chair Simon! (*Laughs.*) . . . Well, it's very nice, Simon: it's always sunny – lots of birds and so forth, plenty of football – and there are no penalties, Simon think of that! . . . The pitches are made of green marzipan. . . . Oh you'd be surprised how much punishment marzipan will take. . . .

E: No, no!

J: And the little streams, Simon, are made of lemonade. . . .

E: No, no, Simon, no cyclamate. Everything's organically grown, all free range. . . . No there are no spiders. . . . What? . . . No, it's just that they have a special place of their own, where they can run about amongst themselves. . . .

J: No, Simon, it isn't wicked to dislike spiders. I don't like them very much myself but I do care about them all, desperately.

E: Yes of course He does! He cares about every single living thing – and that's an awful lot – so you see you mustn't bother God with your guilt. . . . What do you mean, that's not what He said last night?

J: Not what who said? . . . I wasn't here last night. . . . I was *not*. . . .

E: He can be so stubborn when he wants. I think we'd better give it up as a bad job. I'll phone Dr Phillips in the morning.

J: Oh hang it all. Where does he get this guilt from? He makes me feel guilty. I've let him down . . . my only son. Jesus, it makes me wish I'd never been born.

E: I can see where he gets it from, you sound just like your father!

J: My father was a saint . . .

E: Oh let's go to bed – he'll cry himself out.

They leave.

VOICE: Hello Simon. Sorry I'm late. Someone's been taking My Name in vain and I had to go along and sort him out. Now then – where were we? I want you to go to the Children of Israel, and here's the gist of what I want you to say . . .

✣ Children

JOHN *stands uneasily – a stranger in his own home.*

E: Funny – you never brought me flowers when we were married, John.

J: Oh for God's sake Eleanor! It's difficult enough as it is without your being . . .

E: I'm sorry. I don't . . . I can't. . . .

She reaches out her hand to him. He backs a little. She withdraws her hand. He puts his out to her.

Would you like a drink?

J: No thanks.

E: Well sit down. . . . Well. . . . How are things at work?

J: Oh so so.

E: Has Miss Parsons had her baby yet?

J: No she has it at the end of the week I think.

E: Is she going to marry the man?

J: I honestly couldn't say, darling. I've got other things on my mind just at present.

E: Well she won't if she takes my advice.

J: Must you?

E: What? . . . I'm only saying that in my small experience, marriage isn't a very satisfactory institution. For a woman at any rate.

J: Oh come on. . . .

E: What?

J: If you could only hear yourself Eleanor. You're being so boring.

E: Oh? . . . I'm sorry. . . . You don't *have* to come to see me.

J: I haven't come to see you really, have I? I came to see Alexander. Where is he, by the way?

E: Well surely you got my message? Wednesday is his day for finger-painting. . . .

J: Oh God. . . .

E: Surely Miss Parsons told you? She's so efficient.

J: Oh well, I can't have taken it in. . . .

E: It's happened three times in a row. It's almost as if you were trying to avoid him, John.

J: Oh don't be ridiculous Eleanor. . . . That's a pretty dress you're wearing.

E: Really? . . . Oh you're just saying that.

J: Of course I'm just saying it. Do you want me to sing it?

E: No but I know you – the only time you say something nice is when you want something –

J: That's not *true*.

E: I know.

J: Then why did you say it?

ELEANOR *shakes her head.*

J: Look darling – I've been thinking –

E: Gosh you must be tired –

J: No please – I'm serious –

E: Sorry –

J: I've been thinking a lot lately – about Alexander –

E: Oh . . . I hoped perhaps it'd been me.

J: Well . . . in a sense perhaps . . . indirectly. It just seems to me that we've been terribly, terribly selfish.

E: You've always said we're selfish.

J: Well I think it is selfish to deprive young Alexander of the stability and security which a father alone can give him. Gosh – you've read Freud! . . . Unless of course you remarry –

E: I'm not likely to do that!

J: Oh, you never know . . . you're still very attractive. . . .

E: Ch I know. I didn't mean that . . . I was rather in love with you, you know.

J: – Oh come on –

E: You great oaf . . . ! (*She gives him a little shove.*)

J: That's neither here nor there. – There we go being selfish again! Look – don't jump down my throat – I feel it would do Alexander less harm if we sacrificed our own feelings and had another stab at making a go of it – for Alexander's sake. . . .

E: But it was for Alexander's sake we separated in the first place; because of our endless fighting.

J: Funny. Since I've been away I'd rather forgotten all that. The rows. I suppose I – rather selfishly – I only remember the good times.

E: They were good, weren't they? Oh John, when did it all begin to go wrong?

J: I don't know.

E: I do. I can remember when we had our first row. It was over having a baby. You kept on saying how selfish it was to have such a wonderful life and not share it with a child.

J: Yes I remember. And then Alexander came.

E: Yes. And after that we seemed to have more and more rows.

J: Can't blame Alexander for that, mind you.

E: Of course not. I wasn't.

J: Just that you were tired all the time because he didn't stop crying. And I was irritated by the noise and the smell and having to do the cooking; and we seemed to get on each other's nerves the whole time –

E: He was a particularly difficult baby, poor mite.

J: Nothing poor about it. He had everything he wanted. All he did was sleep and eat and scream.

E: You did plenty of screaming yourself, I remember. I think you were jealous of him.

J: Jealous? Of that little nonentity? . . . It's not as if he got any better as he got older.

E: We mustn't be so awful about him. He can be so sweet . . . The other day he asked me – of course – 'Where do babies come from, Mummy?' Little devil. The way he looked at me! I didn't know what to say.

J: From the bloody Adoption Society of course, what else? . . . I wish his father had been impotent like me. . . .

E: No one could be impotent like you, darling –

J: – Oh you know – I mean, sterile. . . . Yes! – And that's another reason why we should stay together. What the hell are we going to tell the Adoption Society?

E: Well frankly, I'd rather do that than go back to the kind of life we've been living; you turning into some kind of unrecognizable monster and me just nagging you more each day.

JOHN *gets up impatiently, begins striding about and falls over some toys.*

After much swearing and comforting, he grabs her. They hug.

J: Oh, darling!
E: What are we going to do?
J: You know what I'd like to do . . .
E: No, darling, it isn't safe.
J: Of course it's *safe.*
E: No, darling – I mean Alexander. He may be home any moment.
J: Damn Alexander! It's all his fault, you know that don't you?
E: Oh you can't be so hard on him. Though I must say he's very vicious about you sometimes. . . . You know he is a little bastard –

J: I know he's a little bastard! They got married, you know –

E: Who?

J: Alexander's parents. Geology students! I ask you. It makes my blood boil to think of them . . . strolling arm in arm picking up ammanites, chipping off bits of this and that . . . while we poor innocents have to put up with that brat. They're laughing! The thing that really drives me screaming up the wall is to think of how selfish they are.

E: We ought to have been able to cope with him, though. He's only a little boy. If we could only assert ourselves –

The doorbell rings. ELEANOR *looks stricken.*

That'll be him!

J (*resolute, defiant, slightly crazed*): Don't answer it.

They sit there fearful. The bell rings again : a prolonged series of long, long rings.

Extra

J: Happy, darling?
E: Yes . . .
   Pause.
J: Darling?
E: Yes?
J: What are you thinking?
E: Oh . . . I was just remembering something you said
   once, about there being three phrases which always
   crop up when an affair's coming to an end.
J: I don't remember.
E: One is: Are you happy, darling? One is: What are
   you thinking? . . . I don't remember what the other
   one was.
J: Tch. Darling . . . I love you.
E: Oh yes. That was it.

He's a homosexual isn't he?
Is he? . . . No . . . don't think so . . . he's heterosexual.
Oh . . . I knew he was something.

In the groves of Academe

E : Who is it?   Who is it?

J : It's me, Mrs Casaubon.

E : Who? John! What does this mean? What are you doing here? How on earth did you get in? Your tutorial isn't until ten. What time is it?

J : Half past five.

E : Is it Wednesday today?

J : No, it's Sunday. I'm a bit early.

E : How dare you!

J : I came to apologize for what I did in the Library yesterday.

E : That's best forgotten. Did you have to break into my bedroom?

J : I couldn't sleep. I kept seeing you, with your head pressed back against the *Statistical Account of Warwickshire*, and hearing you whisper 'Stop it'. I was mad to try and kiss you. I feel I owe you an explanation.

E : You're only making things worse. What if Edward, my husband, were to come in?

J : I thought he'd gone back to Greece.

44

E: Yes he has, but what if he hadn't? I think you'd better go.

J: No, please hear me out. I couldn't bear you to misunderstand what happened. I probably gave you the impression by kissing you that I was attracted to you physically. Did I?

E: John. Don't be a baby. It's very natural. It happens so often that a student gets a crush on his tutor. Don't worry: you'll meet a girl, another student probably . . .

J: No no. You don't understand. Not any girl. What I did was unforgivable. I was using you.

E: What do you mean?

J: I was trying to prove something.

E: What?

He sits on the bed.

Oh!

J: It's all right, Eleanor, you're perfectly safe with me. Don't tell me you haven't heard what they say about me.

E: What?

J (*bitterly*): That I prefer men to women.

E: John. No. . . . I had heard quite the opposite.

J: That's the impression I try to give. That's why I kissed you in the library. I wanted to make a public gesture.

E: But there was nobody else in the library.

J: I planned it rather badly.

E: John. So you're a . . . ?

JOHN *nods.*

Poor John. How brave of you to tell me . . . it's funny. I always felt you were different from the others.

J: Did you?

E: Yes . . . but I never for a moment imagined. . . . What a waste!

J: Waste. Why?

E: You're far and away the most attractive man in your year.

J: I don't know. I find some of the others terribly attractive.

E: Tch! How sad. Do you want to talk?

J: Yes.

E: All right. I'll go and make us some tea, shall I?

J: No no no no! Stay there.

E: What is it?

J: T-tea disagrees with me.

E: Poor boy.

J: What a beautiful nightdress!

E: Oh?

J: Um . . . I've always wanted one like that.

E: Tch!

Pause.

I just can't believe it.

J: What?

E: You . . . you're so . . . (*Strokes his head.*) I'm sorry, that must be awful for you.

J: No no. Don't stop! . . . Er – It reminds me of my mother. . . .

E: Oh . . . of course . . . There. . . .

J (*his head upon her breast, casting about*): Do you miss Edward?

E: Who? Oh . . . yes.

J: I do terribly.

E: Oh, I see.

J: Yes. That's what draws me to you.

E: Do you find him attractive then?

J: Oh!

E: Oh. Tell me why, what?

J: Is that where he sleeps?

E: Well no. He sleeps in his study. He likes to be near his books.

J: Ah!

E: John.

J: Yes.

E: I don't know how to say this. . . . Well . . . do you regret – I mean, would you like to be . . .

J: Normal?

E: Well, yes.

J: Oh, I wish I were.

E: Have you ever tried?

J: Yes.

ELEANOR *shakes her head.*

JOHN *shakes his head.*

E: Perhaps they were too young for you. I've read about women 'redeeming' homosexuals.

J: Yes.

E: What you need is someone older, very experienced.

J: Perhaps.

E: What a pity.

J: Why?

E: I wish I could think of someone.

J (*panic*): Why??

E: You're so worth helping. I'd be tempted to try myself but it's no good.

J: Why not?

E: I'm not experienced enough.

J: What about Edward?

ELEANOR *makes a grimace.*

J (*a moment of despair*): Oh God. It's no good. I suppose I'm doomed.

E: Oh don't say that. If I thought there was any chance . . . but my body would just disgust you.

J: Disgust is too strong a word. I can see that you must be attractive – looking at it objectively, that is – through your nightdress. Your nightdress . . . it's as plain as a pikestaff – ooh.

E: What's the matter?

J: You've got such boyish shoulders.

E: John.

J: Yes. . . .

E: If you could bring yourself to. . . .

JOHN *is already undressing.*

I'd never do this with someone normal. I couldn't be unfaithful to Edward in the normal way for all his shortcomings.

J: I'll turn out the light.

47

E : John ! I thought you said you were a homosexual.

J : It never fails!

✺ Hello again Paris

JOHN *and* ELEANOR *in a hotel bedroom preparing for bed.* JOHN *looks out of the window.*

J: I love Paris in the springtime!

E: I love it in the autumn too.

J: But spring is really the time for love. . . . Romance.

E: Yes. Perhaps we should have put the wedding off until next spring.

J: No – I couldn't wait to marry you. And it's so glorious to be in Paris with someone who loves it as much as I do.

E: It wasn't actually this hotel you spent your first honeymoon in, was it?

J: Oh no. A little place on the Left Bank. Noisy as hell, but lovely people. . . . Every time I think of that honeymoon I shudder. . . .

E: Poor John!

J: You really don't mind coming to Paris, after . . .

E: Now, John – stop worrying about me! You're supposed to be thinking a bit more about yourself – remember? If you do anything that makes me unhappy – I'll shout, and the same goes for you. Promise? Now go on – you'd better use the bathroom first. I take ages. This is going to be a real honeymoon. . . .

J: That one certainly wasn't.

E: Was it so awful, darling?

J: Appalling . . . Liz got into a complete panic, kept on crying and saying her life was over . . . all her life

49

she'd been waiting to get married and now she
was . . .

E: Were you a virgin, darling?

J: Practically, yes. Were you?

E: Yes. Was she?

J: Yes. Edward?

E: Yes. . . .

E:⎱At least we haven't got all that to go through
J:⎰ again . . .

E: How old was she?

J: Nineteen.

E: Och . . . I was eighteen . . . I wish it could have been
you . . . But I'm very glad it wasn't. God – when I
think of the mistakes I made. . . .

J: You couldn't have been any worse than me. Or Liz
for that matter.

E: Or Edward. . . . The great thing about getting
older . . .

J: Tch, darling. . . .

E: Well, I am. . . .

J: Thank God.

E: Yes, exactly. The great thing about getting older is
that you see things clearly. I see you. You see me.

J: Hello!

E: What is it? Is there someone there?

J: No. I was just saying hello . . .

E: Oh . . . hello. Damn, I've lost my train of thought . . .

J: Sorry. . . .

E: I was just saying . . . it's so wonderful not to *feel*
things so deeply . . . God knows I love you, but I was
crazy about Edward . . .

J: So you've said. . . .

E: Oh. What a difference . . . chalk and cheese. You're
so solid, safe . . . Edward was so unreliable . . . apart
from everything else. . . .

J: You're not like Liz either . . . but even if you were
like her – I've changed. Even if you did have that –
oh – I don't know . . . you wouldn't be able to put me
through it the way Liz did . . . because I'm older
now . . . Now all I want to do is make someone
happy . . .

E: Well, that's what life's about really, isn't it? (*Knock at the door*.) That'll be the tea. I'll go . . .

J: No, no, no – I'll go. . . . Did you order some?

E: No, let me . . . I thought it would be nice . . . I'll go . . . Oh, no. Perhaps you'd better . . . I've only got this on. . . .

J: *Merci mademoiselle*. . . . Here you are. . . .

E: Are you glad you married me?

J: Of course I am.

E: You've changed a lot already. I must be good for you. When you were with Liz, you looked so . . . pinched . . .

J: She used to pinch me. . . .

E: She never understood you . . . I mean I only met her for five minutes, but it stood out a mile. Even I know you don't take sugar in your tea. She'd been married to you for fifteen years. . . .

J: Well I think you made her a bit nervous – coming round to collect the sheets.

E: Well, they were yours darling. As one gets older one does learn not to let people take advantage. There you are, darling – no sugar for you!

J: I won't have tea, thank you.

E: Oh, you'd rather have had chocolate . . . yes you would. Let me ring down for some.

J: No, no, don't be silly. Changed my mind. I *will* have a cup of tea, precious.

E: One lump or two?

J: Can I have a spoon?

JOHN *fishes out two lumps of sugar.*

E: You know when I first became aware that everything I had ever felt for Edward was dead?

J: Mmm?

E: Oh, it's going to sound so trivial . . .

J: Go on. . . .

E: Well, Edward always hated the dark meat of chicken – just wouldn't eat it. Well, I prefer the breast too – but because I just adored him it always gave me a particular sort of warm feeling to give him the white meat – even more, because he never noticed . . . Anyway, one Sunday I made roast chicken for lunch – and suddenly I thought: what

51

the Hell? and I put some of the dark meat on his plate and some of the white meat on mine – and that really was the beginning of – well, the divorce.

J: Divorce! God, I used to loathe the idea – and yet it has really changed my life.

E: Yes – you're married to me now!

J: No – I just meant it really was the end of my adolescence.

E: I used to hate it too but I don't think that a marriage can be complete without divorce. One only *really* marries once – and that's when you marry for the second time.

J: Absolutely.

E: Marriage is still so valid. Otherwise, living alone makes one so self-absorbed and set in one's ways – like my cup of tea . . . I always have it – oh I didn't know you smoked. . . .

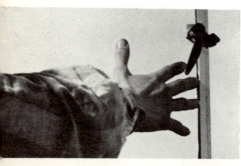

J: I don't. Just a pipe before I turn in. (ELEANOR *opens the window.*) 'Course we've never actually spent a night together, have we? Just the afternoons . . .

E: Let's make our marriage an exciting marriage, shall we?

J (*getting into bed*): I'll try. . . .

E: Don't try. Just be yourself – remember?

JOHN *gets out of bed and closes the window.*

Marriage is the only civilized way to live – I realized that, living alone when Edward left me. It's not only sex and companionship – but there are certain things that one shouldn't have to do – getting taxis – ordering wine. Oh – do you sleep on that side?

J: Yes – I can't bear to sleep on the other side – do you mind?

E: Oh – I usually sleep on that side.

J: Oh – do you?

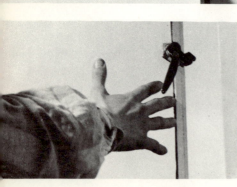

E: Doesn't matter . . . (*She opens the window.*) Of course, there are things a woman does better than men – turn out the light darling. . . .

J: Like washing shirts. God, I'll be glad to be shot of that ghastly laundry. . . .

E: Oh, it's so good not to be alone any more . . . I used to get quite frightened sometimes in the night. . . . What shall we do tomorrow darling? I'll be going shopping in the morning, and seeing Madame Roussel in the afternoon. . . . Darling?

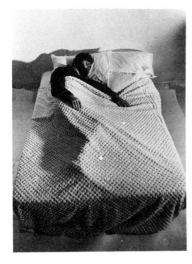

Tch! Asleep.

Oh well, in
that case . . .

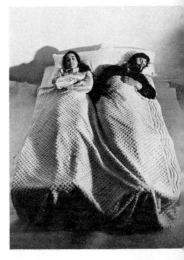

. . . might as well be comfy.

Instead

✤ Picnic

Wind and weather and sea, a car parked. JOHN *is in the headlights, busy with a fire.* ELEANOR *comes from the car with a picnic hamper.*

J: Sorry – do you want a hand with that?

E (*stumbling*): Sorry . . . it's so inky. I can hardly see. No thanks, I think I can manage . . . You must be worn out after all that driving. (*She kneels by the fire and starts unpacking.*)

J: Look here. Are you positive you wouldn't prefer to eat in the car?

E: Oh no! That wouldn't be a picnic at all, would it? Besides look at your lovely fire – you are clever.

J: Mmm. Yes. It did take rather longer than I calculated. I ought to have got a route from the AA.

E: It really doesn't matter. One hardly expects a professor of logic to be a map-reader!

J: All the same – it shouldn't have taken five hours to come the last eighteen miles.

E: Not to worry. I enjoyed it while it was still light.

J: Yes. It's a pretty county, Sussex.

E: Yes. Kent, actually.

J: Oh? Oh . . . perhaps that's why it took us so long.

E: Not to worry. We're here now . . . where is it?

J (*walks away a few paces*): It's just . . .

E: Careful! . . . Do be careful. Don't get too near the edge. . . .

He returns.

How high is it?

J: Oh about just over three hundred and fifty feet I think.

E: How long will it take us to get to the bottom? Roughly.

J: Roughly . . . well . . . as the crow flies. . . . (*They laugh.*) Well. It's thirty-two feet per second per second . . . I'm not very strong on maths. . . .

E : . . . Tch. Oh I'm sure that's not true. . . .

J (*eating a sandwich*): I think that's the figure. I'm not certain what per second per second means but well, thirty-two into three hundred and fifty – well let's say approximately nine seconds.

E : Nine seconds. How long is that? One . . . two . . .

J : No. It's a bit faster than that. (*Looking at his watch.*) One . . . two . . . three . . .

E (*joins in*: . . . four . . . five . . . six . . . seven . . . eight . . . nine. Yes. Oh well. That's not bad, is it? . . . Good. Now . . .

J : You've hardly eaten anything. These are excellent by the way.

E : Oh. Thank you . . . Oh. How silly . . . I forgot . . . would you like a drink?

J : Now let me do that. (*He reaches across to the hamper.*) Name your poison.

E : Oh dear I'm sorry. I didn't bring any spirits. Just some wine. Do you mind? (*He is getting it out, opening it.*) The man said it was awfully good.

J : Perfect. 1953 . . . oh well. Coincidence. That was the year I got my PhD.

E : There you are. They said it was a good year . . . but Heavens . . . 1953 . . . I hope I'm not being personal . . . but – you must have been a baby. . . .

J (*shrugs and smiles*): Well . . . Well! (*Raising his cup.*) Here's to us!

They drink.

E : Just think . . . all these years you've been lecturing just around the corner, and I had no idea. If I hadn't seen that advertisement about it in the tube . . . I usually take the bus, you see, that's what's so extraordinary, but it was pouring with rain and there was *such* a queue and of course all the buses are full by the time they get to my stop anyway – I've waited sometimes half an hour – and then of course you get five at once . . .

J : Yes . . . yes, you told me . . .

E : Oh, I'm sorry. It was wonderful – it made me feel like that poem by Sassoon – do you know?

'Everyone suddenly burst out singing
'And I was filled with such delight
'As 'prisoned birds must find in Freedom
'Winging wildly across the white . . .'

J (*interrupts*): Yes. Poetry is – to me – an evasion, I'm afraid . . . (*Pause.*) Sorry. I didn't mean to be abrupt. When one has spent one's life considering the absurdity of Existence one tends at times to be a little brusque. I'm not used to speaking to people, you see; only lecturing . . . It was very rewarding for me to find, finally, one student with sufficient imagination and understanding to grasp the implications of what I was saying.

E: Oh it was superb! Suddenly, for me, to feel that suicide was a real possibility, not just an idle dream!

J: Thank you.

E: What I couldn't believe . . . was that *I* could be of any help to someone as – well . . . like you. . . .

J: On the contrary. I'm very grateful to *you* for making all this possible for me. I've always stressed you see that suicide should never be a cowardly rejection of Life. It must be, it has to be, an affirmation of Suicide. That is why the solitary.suicide is meaningless; there must be a witness.

E: Oh dear. When I hear you, I sometimes wonder whether I'm killing myself for the right reasons. I haven't got the brain to think things out like you have. I just want to die . . . but I would never have had the courage to do it on my own – and I didn't have any friends . . . I made such a silly mistake once, did I tell you?

J: What?

E: I heard about this group of people you can phone if you want to commit suicide; so I plucked up my courage – it took me all evening – I kept putting it off and putting it off . . . I am such a coward!

J: What happened?

E: Oh. Well – I phoned – and they tried to talk me out of it!

J: Typical!

56

E: Yes. What I wanted was some encouragement! (*They laugh.*) I was getting really desperate. Every morning I used to look at my gas stove and think: I wonder if it's going to be you. But oh . . . I just couldn't.

J: Yes. Only natural. But you know it's a rotten way to go. (*He drinks.*) Mmm, this is a nice wine.

E: Yes. (*They drink, making appreciative noises.*) It is nice, isn't it. It seemed an awful lot for such a little bottle . . .

J: No. Nonsense . . .

E: But it is worth it I think, isn't it? I must say – I enjoyed preparing this picnic more than anything I've done for – oh years and years and years. . . .

J: Good. Well, it's jolly good.

E: It was marvellous to have . . . oh . . . such a feeling of purpose. . . . In fact the whole of the last week has been like that: such fun! I don't think I shall ever forget it.

J: Yes, it has been fun. I thought I should quarrel with your choice of entertainment last night; but I found, to my surprise that I thoroughly enjoyed it. What was it called again?

E: *The Sound of Music.*

J: I found it was very interesting. I thought its analysis of the Nazi ideology in 1935 was rather simplistic, but the music was very tuneful. . . .

E: I wanted to see it because of the nuns . . . do you know I've never been to the theatre? I didn't like to on my own.

J: That was the cinema.

E: Of course, yes. It was so generous of you to take me. And the dinner afterwards. It was so beautiful. That lovely room . . . and after what we had said about going Dutch.

J: Nonsense – my pleasure. It's nice to lash out once in one's life.

E: Have you had enough?

J: Oh yes. Thank you. Moderation in all things. Yes . . . well. This won't do. . . .

E: Oh! Yes. Rightyho.

They return the things to the hamper and the hamper to the car. JOHN *turns out headlights. They meet again at the fire.*

J: Ready?
E: Yes.

They walk a short way together.

J: Well – Goodbye, Eleanor. Thank you for everything.
E: Oh! Thank you! . . . If I may say so: it has been such a privilege to know you and . . .
J: Not at all . . . goodbye.
E: Goodbye . . . Oh! Em, John, I . . . Oh sugar . . .

There is a splash and shortly after : another splash.

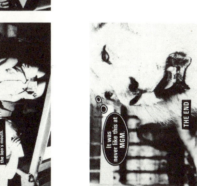

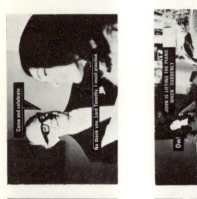